INSECTS

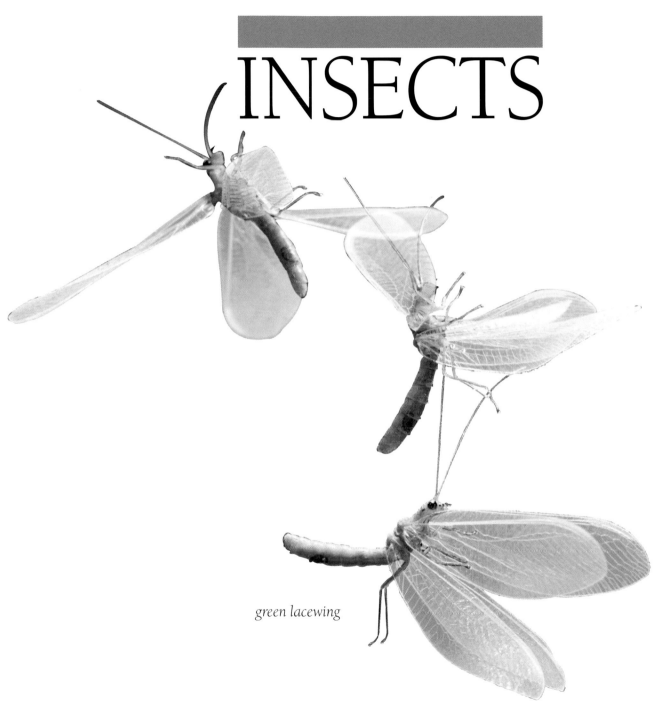

green lacewing

NATIONAL GEOGRAPHIC NATURE LIBRARY

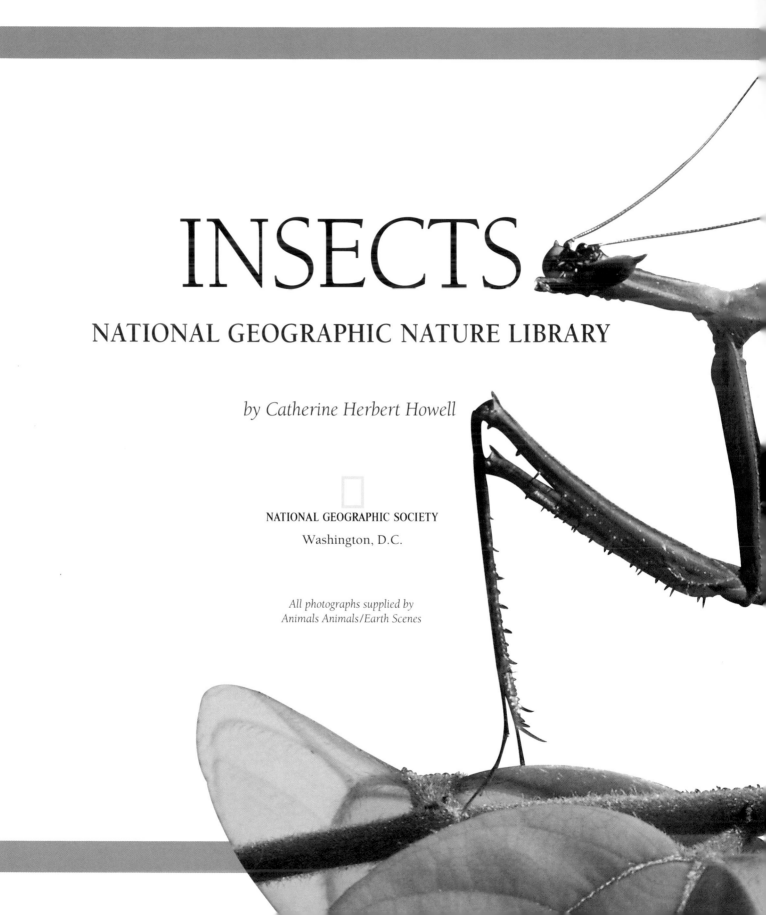

INSECTS

NATIONAL GEOGRAPHIC NATURE LIBRARY

by Catherine Herbert Howell

NATIONAL GEOGRAPHIC SOCIETY

Washington, D.C.

*All photographs supplied by
Animals Animals/Earth Scenes*

slender flower mantis

Table of Contents

atlas moth

WHAT IS AN INSECT? 6

Here, There, and Everywhere 8

Inside Out 10

Bits and Pieces 12

Munch Bunch 14

What Is Not an Insect 16

earwig

1 Old-timers 18

2 Crickets and Kin 20

The Legs Have It! 22

leaf katydid

3 Mantises and More 24

giant water bug

4 Bug Bytes 26

Baby Buggies 28

5 Butterfly Basics 30

Changing Times 32

Monarchs on the Move 34

Moth Magic 36

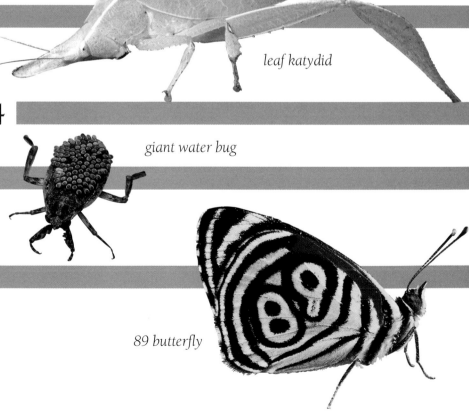

89 butterfly

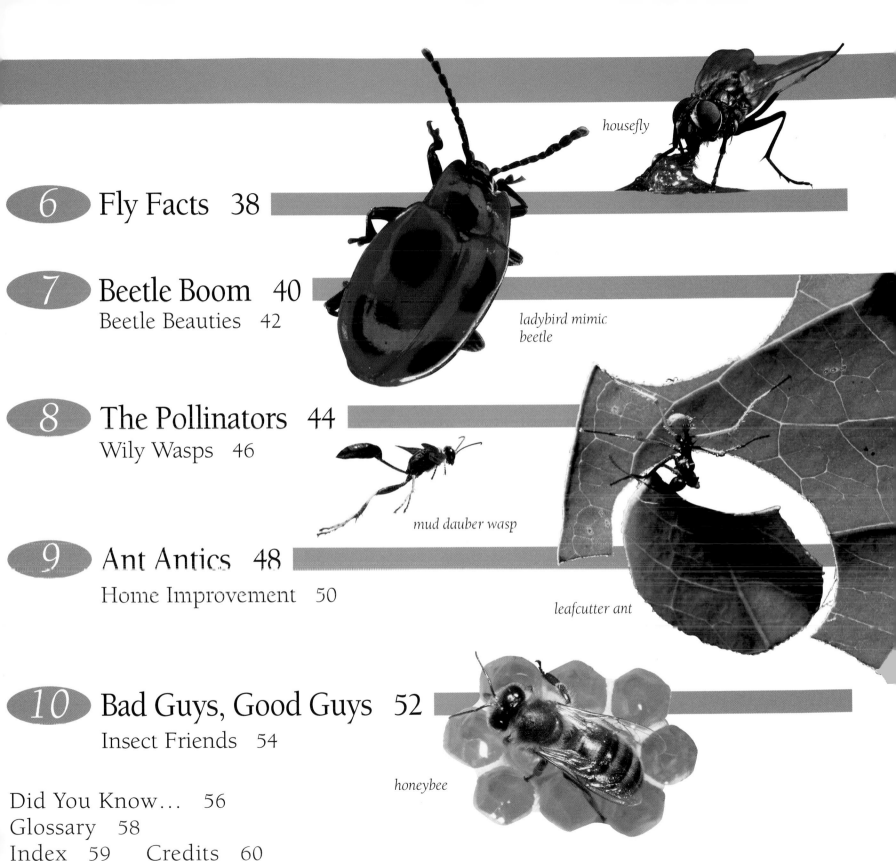

6 Fly Facts 38

7 Beetle Boom 40
Beetle Beauties 42

8 The Pollinators 44
Wily Wasps 46

9 Ant Antics 48
Home Improvement 50

10 Bad Guys, Good Guys 52
Insect Friends 54

Did You Know… 56
Glossary 58
Index 59   Credits 60

housefly

ladybird mimic beetle

mud dauber wasp

leafcutter ant

honeybee

5

WHAT IS AN INSECT?

Insects are the animals you probably meet most often. They form the world's largest animal group. There are more than a million known species, or kinds, of insects. Scientists place similar insects into about 30 large categories, called orders.

An ant and a butterfly may seem very different, but they are both insects and have these insect features:

- They BREATHE AIR.
- They are INVERTEBRATES (in-VURT-uh-bruts).
- They have a SKELETON ON THE OUTSIDE OF THE BODY.
- Their bodies have THREE SEGMENTS.
- They have THREE PAIRS OF LEGS.
- Many have ANTENNAE AND WINGS.
- Most hatch from EGGS AND MAY CHANGE FORM SEVERAL TIMES.

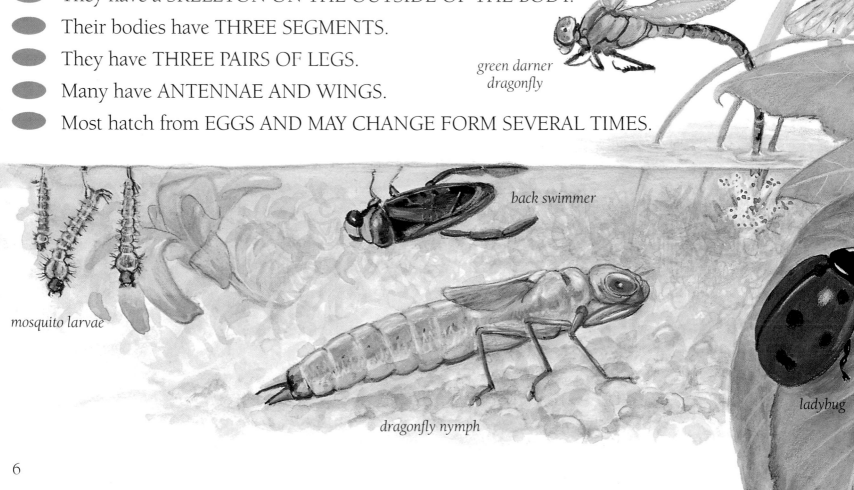

greenbottle fly

green darner dragonfly

back swimmer

mosquito larvae

dragonfly nymph

ladybug

6

bumblebee

praying
mantis

eastern tiger
swallowtail butterfly

grasshopper

aphids

eastern tiger
swallowtail
caterpillar

male stag beetles

black ants

7

Here, There, and Everywhere

Insects thrive on all seven continents and in every kind of habitat. They live in and on the ground, in water, and in the sky. Some insects even survive in puddles of oil. New species of insects are discovered all the time. Some insects are smaller than the period at the end of this sentence. Others are bigger than a dinner plate. Some insects, such as the mayfly, live only a few hours; others, such as the queen termite, can have a life span of 50 years.

A special forked prong on its abdomen, usually kept folded under the body, propels the springtail into the air. Springtails, one of the first insects on earth, lack wings.

MOVE OVER

A square mile of field may be home to more than 5.5 billion insects, a number equal to the world's human population. That field would include beetles, crickets, and caterpillars, but it would shelter more springtails than any other type of insect—about half a billion.

MEGAMOTH

With a wingspan of up to 12 inches, the atlas moth lives in the foothills of the Himalaya and elsewhere in southeastern Asia. The front wing tips of the atlas moth resemble a snake's head, one way the moth scares off enemies. It would take thousands of eulophid (you-LOAF-id) wasps, one of the world's smallest insects, to cover the wing area of the atlas moth.

A eulophid wasp is less than an eighth of an inch long.

0 1

eulophid wasp

Smooth, scaleless patches on the wings of the atlas moth may reflect light and warn off predators.

Inside Out

Insects have skeletons on the outside of their bodies. This exoskeleton, meaning "outside skeleton," is made of a strong, light material called chitin (KIE-tin). Chitin contains protein, as your hair does, which is flexible enough to let insects creep, crawl, jump, fly, and even swim. An insect's body is divided into three main parts, or segments—head, thorax, and abdomen.

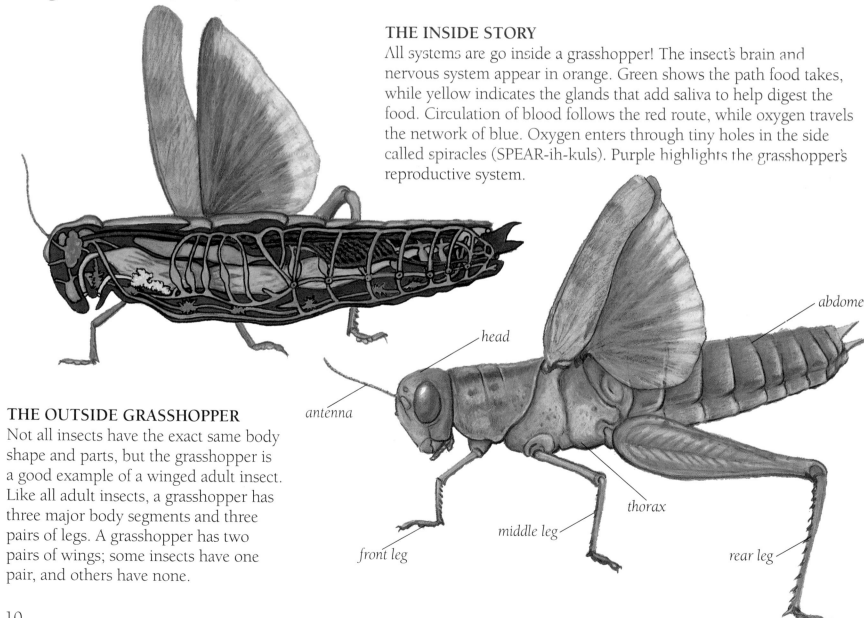

THE INSIDE STORY

All systems are go inside a grasshopper! The insect's brain and nervous system appear in orange. Green shows the path food takes, while yellow indicates the glands that add saliva to help digest the food. Circulation of blood follows the red route, while oxygen travels the network of blue. Oxygen enters through tiny holes in the side called spiracles (SPEAR-ih-kuls). Purple highlights the grasshopper's reproductive system.

head

antenna

abdome

thorax

middle leg

front leg

rear leg

THE OUTSIDE GRASSHOPPER

Not all insects have the exact same body shape and parts, but the grasshopper is a good example of a winged adult insect. Like all adult insects, a grasshopper has three major body segments and three pairs of legs. A grasshopper has two pairs of wings; some insects have one pair, and others have none.

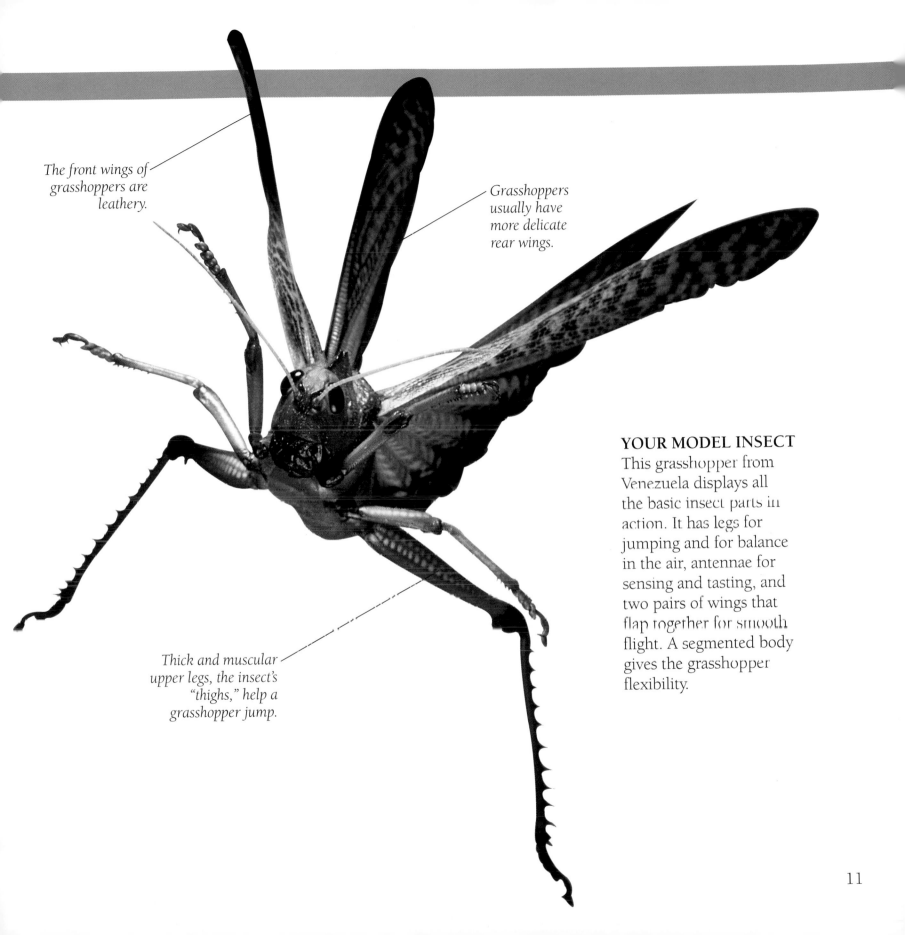

The front wings of grasshoppers are leathery.

Grasshoppers usually have more delicate rear wings.

YOUR MODEL INSECT
This grasshopper from Venezuela displays all the basic insect parts in action. It has legs for jumping and for balance in the air, antennae for sensing and tasting, and two pairs of wings that flap together for smooth flight. A segmented body gives the grasshopper flexibility.

Thick and muscular upper legs, the insect's "thighs," help a grasshopper jump.

Bits and Pieces

Basic body parts can look different from one insect group to another. The dot-like simple eyes of some insects that eat only plants little resemble the compound eyes of insects that hunt for food. Insects change form during their lives, and their body parts change, too. The short, spiky antennae of a moth caterpillar look nothing like the long, feathery ones it wears as an adult moth.

ONE AMONG MANY

Each compound eye is made up of many, often thousands, of six-sided, or hexagonal, facets (FASS-its). Each facet has a hexagonal lens on the surface and another, cone-shaped one inside. The lenses focus light down a rod, where it is passed on as information to the brain.

FINE TUNING

Feathery antennae fan out on each side of a male Chinese oak silk moth's head. Antennae tell insects a lot about their environment—the location and taste of food, and the whereabouts of enemies and possible mates.

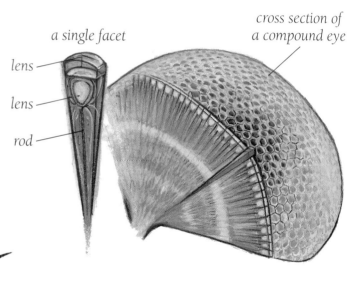

a single facet

cross section of a compound eye

lens

lens

rod

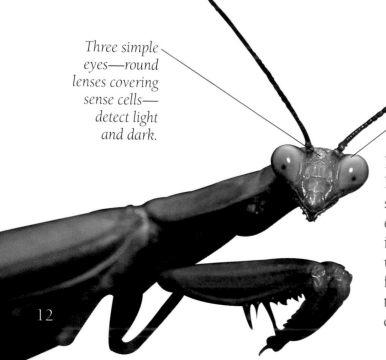

Three simple eyes—round lenses covering sense cells— detect light and dark.

compound eye

DOUBLE VISION

Many insects have both simple and compound eyes. Compound eyes in a head that can move up and down and from side to side spell trouble for the prey of a praying mantis.

EYES OF A DRAGON

Fast-flying hunters like the dragonfly need sharp eyes—and they have them. Shown magnified 32 times, a dragonfly's compound eye can contain an awesome 30,000 facets.

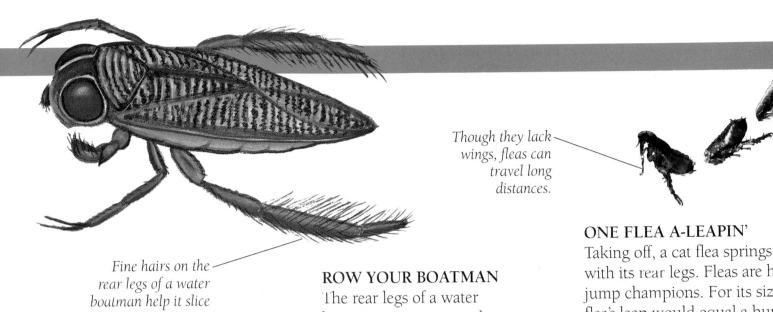

Fine hairs on the rear legs of a water boatman help it slice through the water.

Though they lack wings, fleas can travel long distances.

ROW YOUR BOATMAN
The rear legs of a water boatman serve as oars that move the bug smoothly through the water.

ONE FLEA A-LEAPIN'
Taking off, a cat flea springs up with its rear legs. Fleas are high-jump champions. For its size a flea's leap would equal a human jump of 700 feet.

BUILT TO GO THE DISTANCE
Streamlined and shiny as a race car, a two-striped grasshopper stands ready to jump. These long-legged leapers draw their jointed legs close to their bodies and tighten their muscles before taking off.

Some grasshoppers "sing" by scraping their rear legs against their wings.

13

Munch Bunch

There are many kinds of mouths in the insect world. Different mouths mean that insects feed in different ways. Look at insects that make a meal from plant parts: Leaf-munchers have mouths made for cutting and chewing, while nectar-sippers have straw-like mouthparts. Other insects grab prey in their spiny jaws before settling down to eat. Some insects use their spear-like mouths to pierce a victim and suck fluids from its body.

All mosquitoes and many flies have long, slender mouthparts for piercing and sucking.

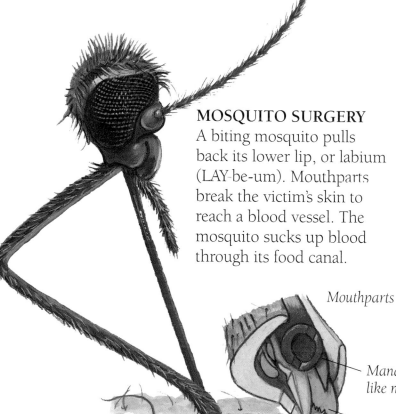

MOSQUITO SURGERY
A biting mosquito pulls back its lower lip, or labium (LAY-be-um). Mouthparts break the victim's skin to reach a blood vessel. The mosquito sucks up blood through its food canal.

Mouthparts

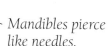

Mandibles pierce like needles.

Maxillae (max-SIL-ee) cut like knives.

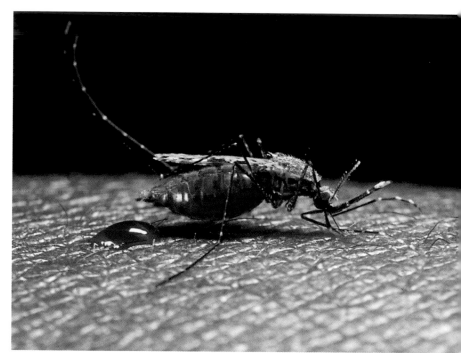

BLOOD BANK
Its abdomen swollen with blood, a mosquito feeds on a human victim. Only the female mosquito drinks animal blood. Protein in the blood helps her eggs develop. Males, and sometimes females, visit flowers to feast on nectar.

When not in use, a butterfly proboscis is tightly coiled.

TOTALLY TUBULAR

A butterfly unrolls its long proboscis (prah-BAH-siss) to reach deep into flowers for nectar. This hollow tube may be longer than the insect's body.

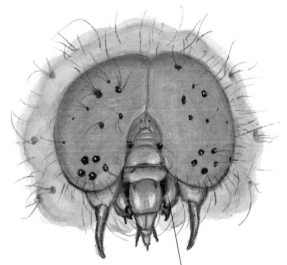

Powerful jaws used for devouring leaves make a caterpillar a long, mean eating machine.

JAWS OF DEATH

A bulldog ant has strong, jagged jaws that help it grasp and kill its prey.

15

What Is Not an Insect

Like insects, the animals on this page are invertebrates called arthropods (ARE-thruh-pods). Some arthropods are often mistaken for insects. Non-insect arthropods such as spiders have a body with *two* segments and *four* pairs of legs. Centipedes and millipedes have many body segments, each with its own legs. Crabs, lobsters, and shrimp usually have five pairs of legs and two sets of antennae.

A crab's front pair of legs end in grasping pincers. Its little abdomen curls forward beneath its body.

DOUBLE THE FUN

A millipede has two sets of legs on each segment of its body. Centipedes have only one pair of legs on each body segment. The word millipede means "one thousand legs," but the average millipede has only about 30 pairs of legs. In the tropics millipedes may grow to be a foot long.

The burrowing wolf spider hunts by night. Three rows of eyes in its head help it spot prey. Under its head are leg-like pedipalps (PEH-dih-palps) that function as feelers.

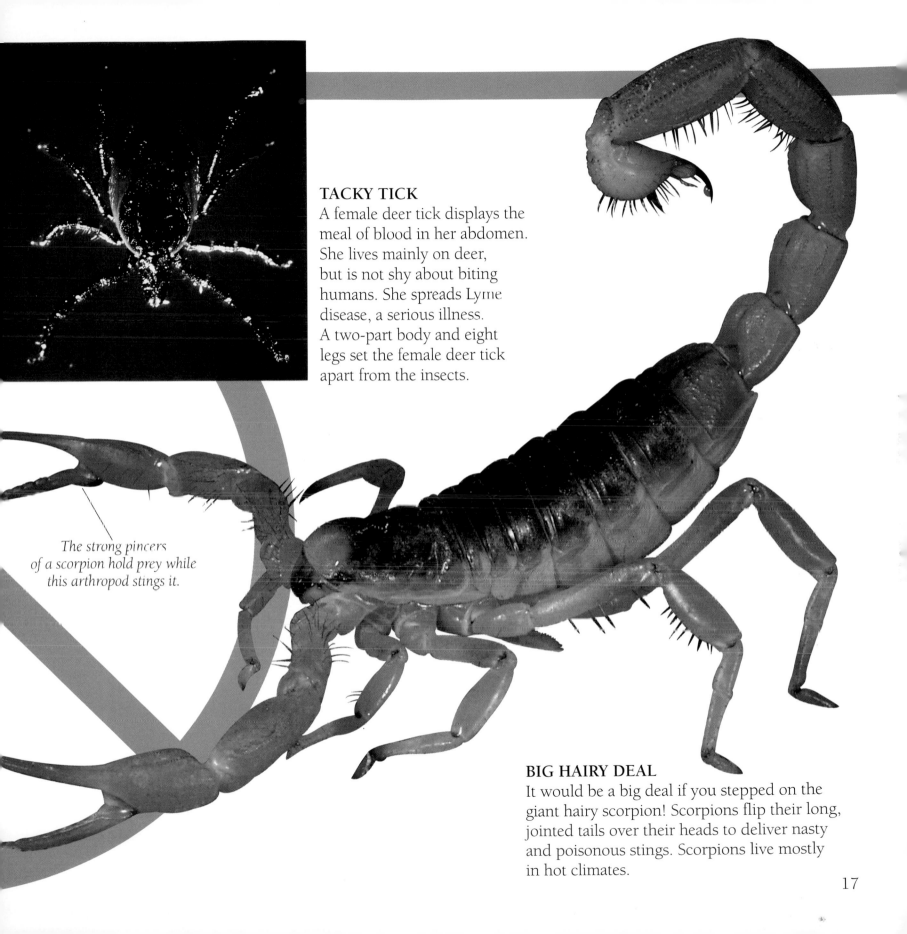

TACKY TICK
A female deer tick displays the meal of blood in her abdomen. She lives mainly on deer, but is not shy about biting humans. She spreads Lyme disease, a serious illness. A two-part body and eight legs set the female deer tick apart from the insects.

The strong pincers of a scorpion hold prey while this arthropod stings it.

BIG HAIRY DEAL
It would be a big deal if you stepped on the giant hairy scorpion! Scorpions flip their long, jointed tails over their heads to deliver nasty and poisonous stings. Scorpions live mostly in hot climates.

17

Old-timers

Insects are the true survivors of the animal kingdom. They crawled, hopped, and flew over the earth long before dinosaurs appeared. The first animals to fly, insects developed wings more than three hundred million years ago. Many insects of today closely resemble both winged and wingless insects of ancient times.

DRAGON OF EDEN
Frozen in stone, a dragonfly from the Jurassic period shared the earth with dinosaurs. Some ancient dragonflies had wingspans stretching 30 inches from tip to tip.

Sharp pincers and a nasty smell help an earwig defend itself.

Almost a twin of the fossil above, a modern dragonfly displays the strong wings that make it an aerial acrobat.

LEND AN EAR
People once believed the earwig invaded sleepers' ears to bite them.

ROACH MOTEL
Hissing cockroaches hang together, perhaps for warmth. One of the oldest and most successful of insect groups, cockroaches eat almost anything, including paper, glue, and clothing.

Dragonflies today rarely have wingspans of larger than six inches.

ZAPPED IN SAP ▶
A midge—a type of fly—trapped in amber, or fossilized pine sap, met its end with a mite on its back. The mite, an arthropod but not an insect, fed on the small fly's blood.

2 Crickets and Kin

You usually hear them before you see them. On summer nights crickets and grasshoppers can fill the darkness with chirping songs. Only males sing, but females pay close attention to these mating calls. Many insects, including crickets and grasshoppers, depend on camouflage—or looking like a part of their environment—to hide from predators.

HOT FOOT
Feet that act like snowshoes keep the dune cricket from sinking into the sand of its desert home. A see-through body helps the cricket blend with its surroundings.

A cricket nymph has all its adult traits, except for size, wings, and the ability to mate.

A CRICKET GROWS UP
To get from egg to adult, a cricket goes through several changes in form, a process known as metamorphosis (meh-tuh-MOR-fuh-sis). The egg hatches into an immature cricket, called a nymph (NIMF). A nymph grows and breaks out of its exoskeleton four or more times. This process is called molting. When a cricket reaches the adult stage, growth stops. The entire transformation takes about six weeks.

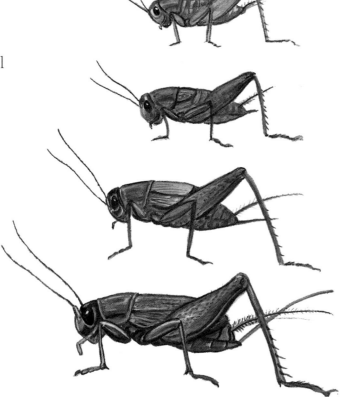

LEAF ME ALONE
A kind of grasshopper, the leaf katydid mimics plant leaves to hide from predators, such as birds. Katydids live high in trees. They got their name from the sound of the males' calls.

The katydid's leaf act is complete, right down to the veins in its side.

The Legs Have It!

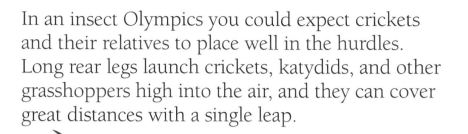

In an insect Olympics you could expect crickets and their relatives to place well in the hurdles. Long rear legs launch crickets, katydids, and other grasshoppers high into the air, and they can cover great distances with a single leap.

A beard-lichen grasshopper's long legs allow this "plant" to leap great distances.

LICHEN LOOK
The beard-lichen (LY-kun) grasshoppe[r] from Costa Rica wea[rs] an intricate plant-lik[e] pattern. It blends wi[th] the foliage in the tropical forests there[.]

I COME IN PEACE—NOT!
Looking like an alien, the spiny katydid threatens possible enemies. Spiny katydids live in the rain forests of Central and South America.

Spines on its legs make this katydid look fierce and can do major damage in a fight.

GOTCHA!
Missing its chance to leap away, a cricket becomes a meal for a crab spider.

A female cricket hears a male's love song through an ear, called a tympanum (TIMP-a num), on each front leg. The male cricket "sings" by scraping his front wings together.

LAST RESORT
A frightened grasshopper from Ghana wiggles its striped abdomen while showing off its colorful wings to remind enemies that it tastes horrible.

The colors yellow and black warn other animals that an insect is dangerous.

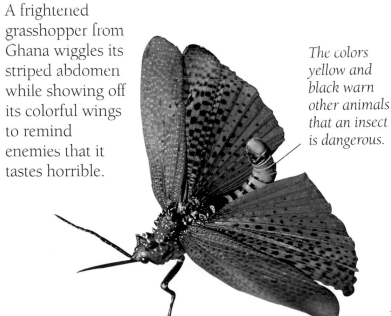

23

3 Mantises and More

The praying mantis got its name from the way it folds its front legs together. It looks as if it's praying, but it's really preying. This meat-eating insect, like all mantises, is a ferocious predator. It waits quietly, twisting its long, flexible body and moveable head. Some mantises look like flowers and other plants to trick the insects they eat. Their cousins, the stick insects, are masters of disguise, too.

This walking-stick's antennae are nearly as long as its wingless body.

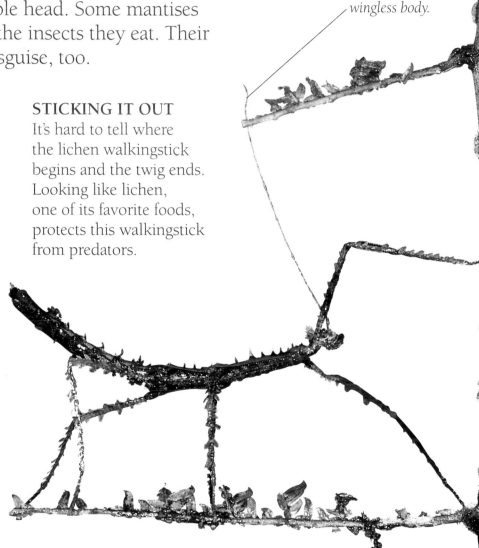

STICKING IT OUT
It's hard to tell where the lichen walkingstick begins and the twig ends. Looking like lichen, one of its favorite foods, protects this walkingstick from predators.

RARE ORCHID
Before it reaches adulthood, an immature flower mantis spends time looking like an orchid. It waits for an unsuspecting bee or butterfly to come within reach. As an adult the flower mantis looks like a regular green mantis.

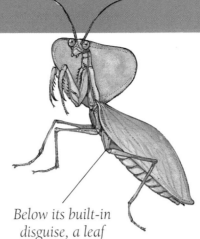

Below its built-in disguise, a leaf mantis has typical insect features.

FEEDING FRENZY
In the right place at the right time, a California mantis snares a hummingbird visiting a feeder. Bird meals are uncommon for a mantis, and this one managed to hang on for only a few minutes before the hummer got away. Mantises live mostly in warm or tropical climates.

HIDE AND SEEK
Look below. Can you find the leaf mantis hidden among the leaves? If you said the insect is the green patch on the left, you're right!

MEAN AND GREEN
A Chinese mantis dines headfirst on a cricket it has trapped. Some mantises also eat each other.

A mantis clings tightly to prey with spiny forelegs.

25

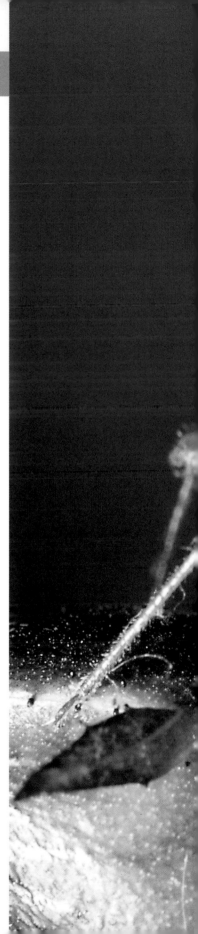

4 Bug Bytes

All bugs are insects, but not all insects are bugs. Fewer than 10 percent of all insects belong to the specific order commonly known as "bugs." They usually have front wings that are thick and hard near the body and thin and clear at the tip. Their rear wings are totally thin and clear. Some bugs eat plants, and others eat insects.

WANTED: DEAD OR ALIVE

A young assassin bug spears a fly with its short beak, then injects a poison. Next the bug will suck the fly's juices and make a tasty meal of the fly. This type of assassin bug is long and thin, like a walkingstick. Other assassin bugs are oval shaped.

IT WALKS ON WATER

A water strider plants its long, slender legs apart and glides across a pond or slow-moving stream. With its weight spread out, it doesn't break the surface of the water and sink.

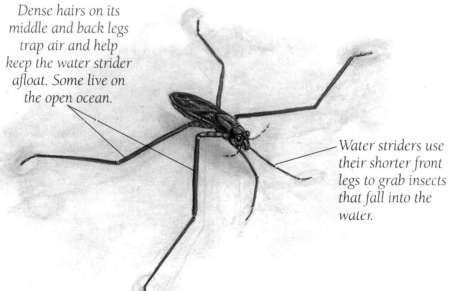

Dense hairs on its middle and back legs trap air and help keep the water strider afloat. Some live on the open ocean.

Water striders use their shorter front legs to grab insects that fall into the water.

eggs

Bugs keep their beaky mouthparts tucked under their bodies when not feeding.

LITTLE STINKER

The harlequin bug is a type of stinkbug. These colorful insects give off a terrible odor when they are disturbed.

Baby Buggies

Bugs and other insects often lay a lot of eggs at one time. Female bugs usually lay their eggs in neat patterns in out-of-the-way places. They are devoted mothers, sometimes guarding the eggs with their bodies. Some bug moms even stay with their young after they hatch to help protect them. Bug dads may help out by "wearing" eggs or by caring for them.

EGGMOBILE
A male giant water bug carries his offspring on his back. A female may stick on more than a hundred eggs that remain for several weeks until hatching.

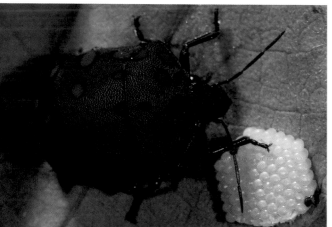

SHIELDING HER YOUNG
A female shield bug, a kind of stinkbug, inspects her eggs. With great care she deposited row after row in a honeycomb pattern on the surface of a leaf. The dotted "shield" on her back may help protect her eggs by warning predators away.

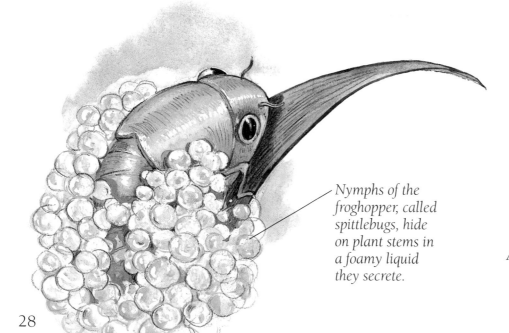

Nymphs of the froghopper, called spittlebugs, hide on plant stems in a foamy liquid they secrete.

Although they lack the spots of adult shield bugs, the nymphs' red color signals predators that they are junior stinkers.

28

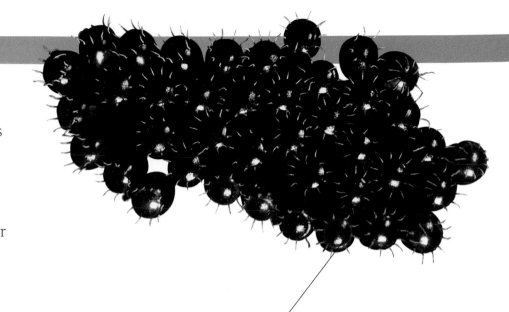

STICKING TOGETHER

After shield bug eggs hatch, the nymphs often cluster in the same place. When an enemy approaches, they may form a circle, facing inward for protection. Many young insects stay together until they grow bigger and stronger and better able to defend themselves.

Some stinkbug eggs look like tiny satellites.

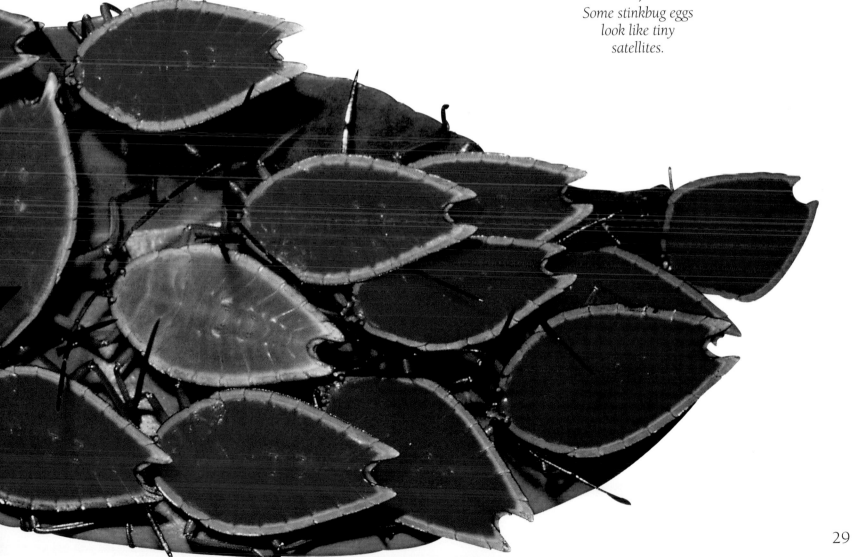

29

5 Butterfly Basics

There is no single way to tell a butterfly from a moth, but there are some pretty common differences. Butterflies are usually more colorful than moths. Butterflies have knobs on the ends of their antennae, while moth antennae are wider and often feathery. At rest butterflies keep their wings closed, while moths usually hold them out flat. Butterflies usually live their lives by day, while most moths are creatures of the night.

WHAT'S IN A NAME?

In flight it hovers like a hawk. As a larva body looks like an elephant's trunk. Wh else to call this insect but an elephant ha moth! Moth wings are usually longer an narrower than butterfly wings.

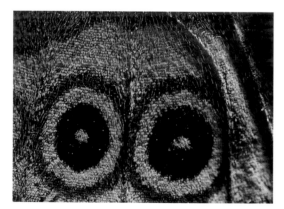

Butterfly and moth wings are formed from tiny, overlapping scales that are powdery and can rub off.

COUNT ME OUT

The 89 butterfly wears its number on its wings. This unusual pattern may confuse attackers.

EYE SPY

Bold circles on a butterfly's wings may startle enemies and keep them away from its head. Known as eyespots, the circles appear on the wings of many butterflies and moths.

Who will be crowned queen of the butterflies? Butterfly wings come i an incredible variety of patterns and colors.

30

Some moths can travel at speeds of 30 miles an hour.

NOTHING SPECIAL

Plainer than most moths, the leaf butterfly doesn't go in for fancy colors. It finds safety in looking like a dry leaf.

CRYSTAL CLEAR

The clear-wing butterfly of Mexico isn't all there. The clear parts of its wings lack scales. See-through wings help it blend with forest scenery, a good thing for these slow-moving insects.

31

Changing Times

For butterflies and moths, each stage of life has a different look. Butterflies and moths take the process of metamorphosis further than crickets and similar insects. Unlike a cricket nymph, the caterpillar that hatches from a butterfly or moth egg looks nothing like the adult insect it will become. The caterpillar is a larva. To get to its adult form, a caterpillar must go through a resting stage. A butterfly caterpillar becomes a chrysalis (KRIH-suh-liss). A moth caterpillar spins itself a cocoon and rests inside as a pupa (PYOO-puh).

FIRST, THE EGG

A monarch caterpillar exits from its ribbed egg. It bit the eggshell to make a hole big enough to squeeze its body through. When totally free, the caterpillar will eat the nutritious shell.

Eating constantly, the caterpillar grows quickly. It sheds its skin several times as it grows.

BASKET OF BUTTERFLIES

When it was time to rest, monarch caterpillars attached themselves to a basket handle. They molted, or shed their skin, for the last time, then each turned into a pale blue-green chrysalis. By the time a butterfly emerges, the chrysalis becomes clear.

Inside the chrysalis, the caterpillar's body parts actually dissolve and re-form as a butterfly.

Its milkweed diet can make a monarch caterpillar poisonous to predators.

Butterflies and moths often lay eggs on their favorite food source so that the larvae will have a ready meal.

When the chrysalis first develops, it is pale blue with gold spots.

STAGES OF LIFE

A monarch follows standard steps from egg to butterfly, a transformation that takes about a month. The growth process is the same for all butterflies. That of moths is similar, but most moth caterpillars transform inside a cocoon they spin from their own silk.

After crawling out of its chrysalis, the new butterfly flexes its wings to pump blood into them.

When its wings are firm and dry, the monarch makes its first flight.

33

Monarchs on the Move

Each fall monarch butterflies undertake an amazing journey. They travel from southern Canada and the northern United States to the mountains of Mexico or the coast of California. Monarchs can travel up to 180 miles a day. They spend the winter in their new locations and then make the long journey home again. Soon after mating, they die.

TIRED AND TATTERED

Flying thousands of miles is rough on a butterfly's wings. Birds cause more damage, pecking at the wings of the exhausted insects. Often, though, the milkweed that monarchs eat as caterpillars helps protect them by making them taste yucky to predators.

A migrating monarch's wings may get as ragged as an old blanket.

TAG, YOU'RE IT

Monarchs mate, unaware that they are tagged for study. Several researchers have monarch tracking programs. Researchers rub scales off a butterfly's wing—a painless procedure—and attach a tag. The tag gives an address so the finder of a monarch can report it. Tracking programs are helping unravel the mysteries of butterfly migration.

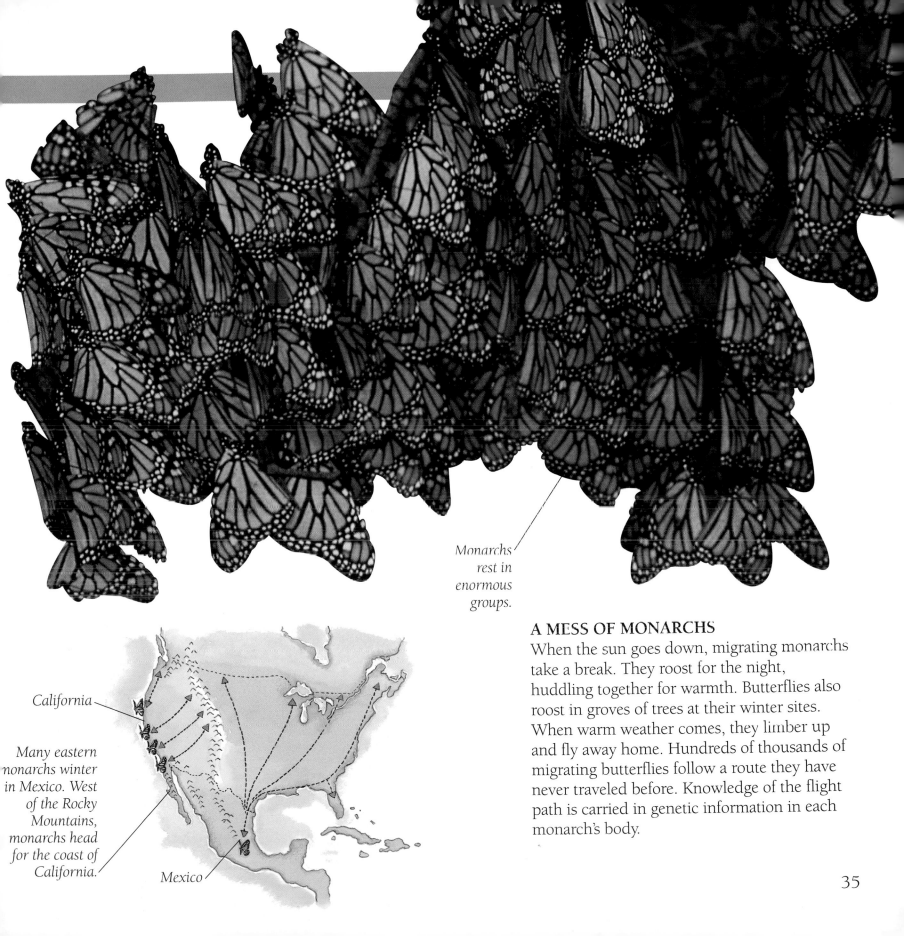

Monarchs rest in enormous groups.

California

Many eastern monarchs winter in Mexico. West of the Rocky Mountains, monarchs head for the coast of California.

Mexico

A MESS OF MONARCHS

When the sun goes down, migrating monarchs take a break. They roost for the night, huddling together for warmth. Butterflies also roost in groves of trees at their winter sites. When warm weather comes, they limber up and fly away home. Hundreds of thousands of migrating butterflies follow a route they have never traveled before. Knowledge of the flight path is carried in genetic information in each monarch's body.

Moth Magic

female · *male*

Male and female moths may differ somewhat in size and wing pattern.

Since most moths are active at night, when it's coolest, their bodies are usually chubbier and furrier than those of butterflies. Often the drab colors moths wear help them hide from predators while they rest on trees during the day. When it's time for a change, many moth caterpillars spin a covering, called a cocoon.

LOVE AT FIRST SIGHT
A moth's life is often short, and some moths mate immediately after hatching. Males of some species hang out around a female's cocoon waiting for her debut.

HANGING TIGHT
A death's-head hawk moth caterpillar hangs from a twig. Its three pairs of true legs lie right below its head. False legs, known as prolegs, and a grasping tail help it get a good grip. The adult death's-head hawk moth sometimes raids beehives to steal honey.

A male moth's antennae can pick up the scent of pheromones (FAIR-uh-moans), or chemicals that attract a mate, from a female moth miles away.

The death's-head hawk moth sports a skull marking that baffles predators.

36

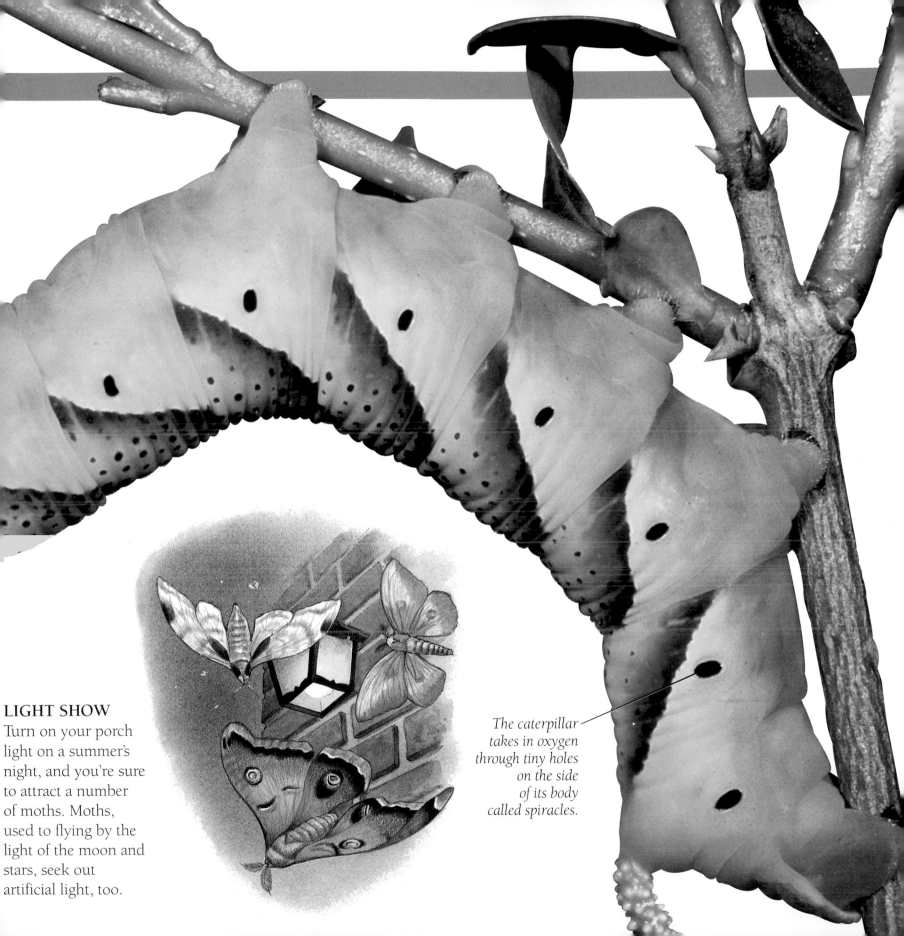

LIGHT SHOW
Turn on your porch light on a summer's night, and you're sure to attract a number of moths. Moths, used to flying by the light of the moon and stars, seek out artificial light, too.

The caterpillar takes in oxygen through tiny holes on the side of its body called spiracles.

6 Fly Facts

Flies are definitely not the most admired of insects. The behavior of some flies—flitting around our heads, biting us and our pets, and landing on our food—is very annoying. Flies often carry germs and diseases because of the places they visit and the ways they feed. They can, however, do some amazing things.

Flies can walk on ceilings and walls because their feet have pads that act as suction cups to grip tight. Flies also use their feet for tasting food.

A yellow dung fly takes to the air with its single pair of wings. A second pair of modified wings serves as a balancing organ. Each modified wing is called a haltere (HALL-tear).

BEE YOURSELF ▶
A syrphid (SUR-fid), or hover, fly looks and acts like a bee, visiting and even pollinating flowers. This mimicry—copycatting a more dangerous insect—helps protect some insects from predators.

A housefly takes its food in liquid form, spitting saliva on sugar to dissolve it, then sucking it up with spongy mouthparts.

SYRPH'S UP
An immature syrphid fly, called a rat-tailed maggot, spends its youth mainly in the water. It sends its "tail," a tube extending from its abdomen, above the surface of water. The "tail" acts as a snorkel and brings air into the insect's body.

38

Beetle Boom

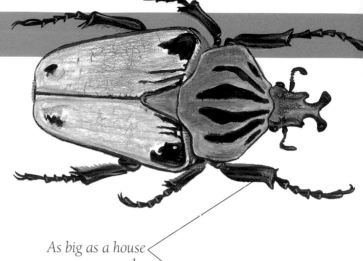

Among insects, there has definitely been a boom in beetles. Beetles are the most numerous insects, with more than 350,000 known species living throughout the world. Beetles are hard-bodied animals. Their firm front wings protect their bodies and their rear wings as well. A beetle egg hatches into a larva called a grub. When the grub is fully grown, it becomes a pupa and rests for a while. After some time, the pupa changes into the adult form of the beetle.

As big as a house sparrow, the goliath beetle of Africa is one of the world's bulkiest insects.

Weevils, some of the weirdest looking beetles, are among the most destructive.

WHEEZING WEEVIL
If beetles got colds, this weevil from Peru would have a tough time. Its snout is nearly as long as its body! A weevil uses its snout to drill into the plants and seeds it eats.

A weevil's jaws lie at the end of its long snout. In some species, so do the eyes.

BEETLE DATE

A male (left) and female (right) stag beetle meet on a log. The male's longer jaws, resembling a stag's horns, help it fight other males to win a mate. Stag beetle bouts may look ferocious, but usually no real harm is done.

When a bombardier beetle feels threatened, it shoots boiling hot toxic liquid at its tormenter. It uses its flexible abdomen to control the direction of the blast.

MOVING MOUNTAINS

Starting with a pile of droppings from a plant-eating mammal, a female dung beetle faces an awesome task. Often the male beetle helps. First, the female fashions the droppings, or dung, into a large ball. Then she patiently rolls the ball to her burrow. On reaching the nest, she pushes the dung in and lays her eggs in it. When the eggs hatch, the larvae will feed on the dung.

41

Beetle Beauties

Colorful and dainty, ladybird beetles—also known as ladybugs—are the sweethearts of the beetle world. They are also some pretty tough customers. Armored with hard wing cases, they taste horrible to predators that can catch them. Ladybugs may be red, orange, or yellow. They may have many spots, or none at all. They help gardeners and farmers by eating pesky aphids (AY-fids) and mites that damage plants and fruit trees.

"Are you my type?" signal male fireflies with their light. Special cells on this beetle's abdomen produce a cool chemical light that blinks in a different pattern for each species.

LET'S SPLIT
An adult ladybug emerges from its pupal shell. Next to it another one waits unhatched, its spots visible through the clear shell.

The wingless females answer with similar blinks.

Ladybird beetles devour aphids by sucking the fluid from their bodies.

COUNT MY SPOTS
Of the more than 3,000 kinds of ladybugs, these beetles have precisely 22 spots on their backs. That's how they got their common name, the 22-dot ladybird.

SNUG AS A LADYBUG
To survive the winter, ladybugs must find a sheltered place to rest. These ladybugs huddle on a tree trunk by the thousands for warmth. When spring comes, they will really warm up and fly away.

LADYBUG WANNABE
Not content with being a beetle, the ladybird mimic beetle passes as that smaller, more compact insect. The mimic's familiar, spotted body may send the message: "Stay away. I taste awful."

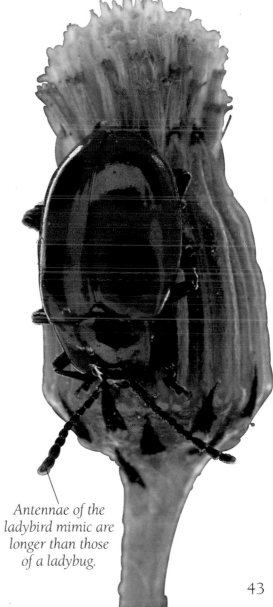

Antennae of the ladybird mimic are longer than those of a ladybug.

43

8 The Pollinators

You may have met a bee the hard way. Many female bees have stingers at the tip of their abdomens and use them when they feel threatened. Bees have furry bodies, usually with a pattern of stripes. Many bees live in colonies, or hives. Bees gather pollen and nectar from flowers for food. They pollinate, or spread pollen, among fruit trees, vegetables, and flowers.

HOME SWEET HIVE

Honeybee colonies may look chaotic, but they are very orderly. The queen is the head bee, producing all the colony's offspring. She mates with male bees, called drones, that die soon after. Female worker bees do all the chores. They tend and feed the queen and her young, build and guard the hive, and make honey from flower nectar.

EAT MY DUST

A honeybee wears the pollen it collects from flowers. It will scrape the pollen onto stiff hairs on its rear legs called pollen baskets and carry it back to the hive. There the pollen will be stored and fed to developing larvae.

The pollen on a bee's fuzzy hairs will brush off on the next flower it visits.

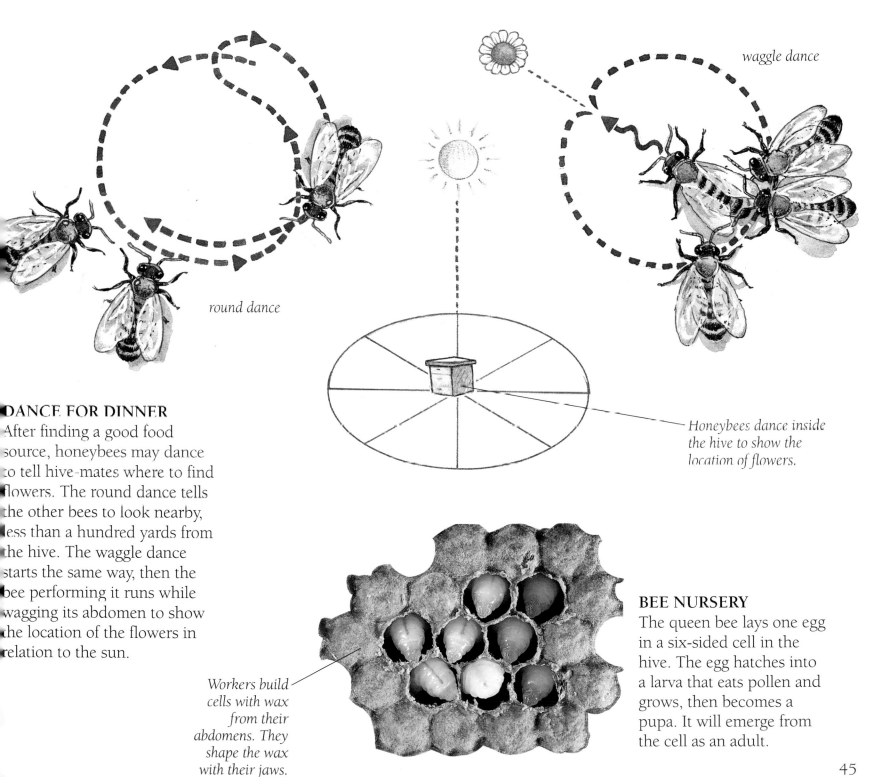

waggle dance

round dance

Honeybees dance inside
the hive to show the
location of flowers.

DANCE FOR DINNER

After finding a good food
source, honeybees may dance
to tell hive-mates where to find
flowers. The round dance tells
the other bees to look nearby,
less than a hundred yards from
the hive. The waggle dance
starts the same way, then the
bee performing it runs while
wagging its abdomen to show
the location of the flowers in
relation to the sun.

*Workers build
cells with wax
from their
abdomens. They
shape the wax
with their jaws.*

BEE NURSERY

The queen bee lays one egg
in a six-sided cell in the
hive. The egg hatches into
a larva that eats pollen and
grows, then becomes a
pupa. It will emerge from
the cell as an adult.

45

Wily Wasps

Wasps are known for their trim waists, the narrow part of the body where the abdomen joins the thorax. Unlike more social bees, wasps often live alone. They build different kinds of elaborate nests. Some claim the nests of other wasps. Many wasps are parasites, laying their eggs in the bodies of other insects and spiders to provide their young with a supply of food.

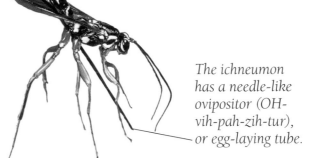

The ichneumon has a needle-like ovipositor (OH-vih-pah-zih-tur), or egg-laying tube.

EGG DRILLER

A female ichneumon (ick-NYOO-mun) wasp uses her long egg-laying tube to lay eggs in another insect's larva. To find the larva, she may probe in wood.

"WAISTING AWAY" ▶

A mud dauber in flight shows off its wasp waist. Mud daubers build large nests of mud cells on walls. The female lays her eggs in a cell stocked with paralyzed insects, then seals it up to keep the food supply safe for her young.

Inside their nests potter wasps store paralyzed caterpillars—food for the larvae when they hatch.

Potters lay their eggs in jug-shaped nests they fashion from mud. Some of the nests are as smooth as pottery made on a wheel.

WEARING WASPS

The braconid (BRAH-cone-nid) wasp lays her eggs in the body of a live hornworm caterpillar. When the eggs hatch, the larvae will eat away at the caterpillar and kill it. Then the larvae crawl outside, spin separate cocoons, and become pupae. One new wasp has already emerged from its cocoon.

47

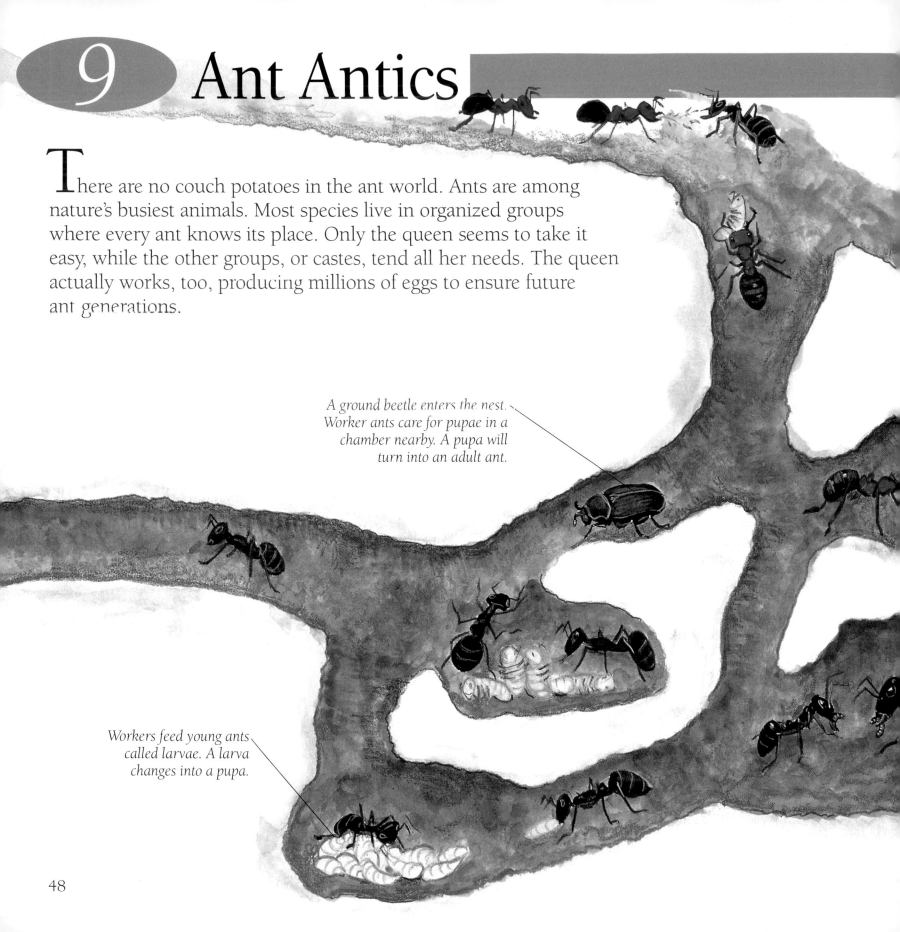

9 Ant Antics

There are no couch potatoes in the ant world. Ants are among nature's busiest animals. Most species live in organized groups where every ant knows its place. Only the queen seems to take it easy, while the other groups, or castes, tend all her needs. The queen actually works, too, producing millions of eggs to ensure future ant generations.

A ground beetle enters the nest. Worker ants care for pupae in a chamber nearby. A pupa will turn into an adult ant.

Workers feed young ants called larvae. A larva changes into a pupa.

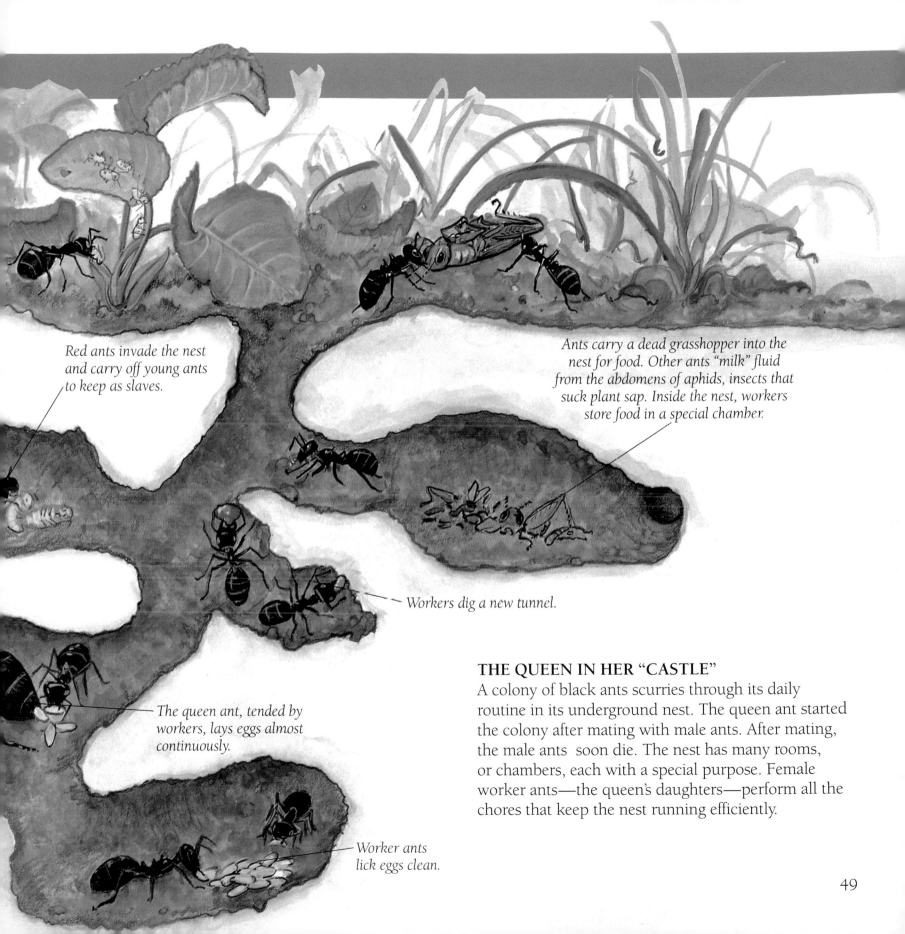

Red ants invade the nest and carry off young ants to keep as slaves.

Ants carry a dead grasshopper into the nest for food. Other ants "milk" fluid from the abdomens of aphids, insects that suck plant sap. Inside the nest, workers store food in a special chamber.

Workers dig a new tunnel.

The queen ant, tended by workers, lays eggs almost continuously.

Worker ants lick eggs clean.

THE QUEEN IN HER "CASTLE"

A colony of black ants scurries through its daily routine in its underground nest. The queen ant started the colony after mating with male ants. After mating, the male ants soon die. The nest has many rooms, or chambers, each with a special purpose. Female worker ants—the queen's daughters—perform all the chores that keep the nest running efficiently.

Home Improvement

Like most ants, leafcutters seldom spend an idle moment. Leafcutters toil tirelessly cutting and transporting leaf and flower pieces to supply their nests with food. These tropical ants repeat the long, tedious chore over and over, but cooperation gets the complex task done.

LEAF PARADE
Worker leafcutters form a ceaseless parade, carrying leaf pieces from treetop to nest. The size of their load is no problem, since ants can easily lift 50 times their own weight. Sometimes another worker hitches a ride on a piece of leaf, possibly as a guard.

Workers heading up the tree often stop to encourage their load-carrying colleagues.

TAKE AN UMBRELLA, DEAR
Leafcutters are also called parasol ants because of the way they hold their leafy burdens over their heads. Parasol ants don't sing in the rain, though. When a shower starts, they stop cutting and return to the nest. Leafcutters destroy rain forest trees and farmers' crops.

Using its scissor-like jaws, a leafcutter worker precisely slices a piece of leaf.

MEANWHILE…
Back at the underground nest, gardener leafcutters drag in leaf pieces left at the entrance by cutters. The gardeners cut the pieces some more and then chew them up. The pulp is placed in special chambers to grow fungus that the colony eats.

51

Bad Guys, Good Guys

Insects exist in such large numbers that their activities have a huge effect on us and on the environment. A swarm of millions of locusts, a kind of grasshopper, can eat through a farmer's field in a few hours. Some mosquitoes and flies spread disease with their bites. Insects can help people, too. Bees and other insects pollinate flowering plants. Insects also provide food and useful materials and help control insect pests.

WHAT A BORE!
Bean weevils use their long snouts to bore into beans to feed. Weevils and other insect pests destroy millions of dollars of food crops annually.

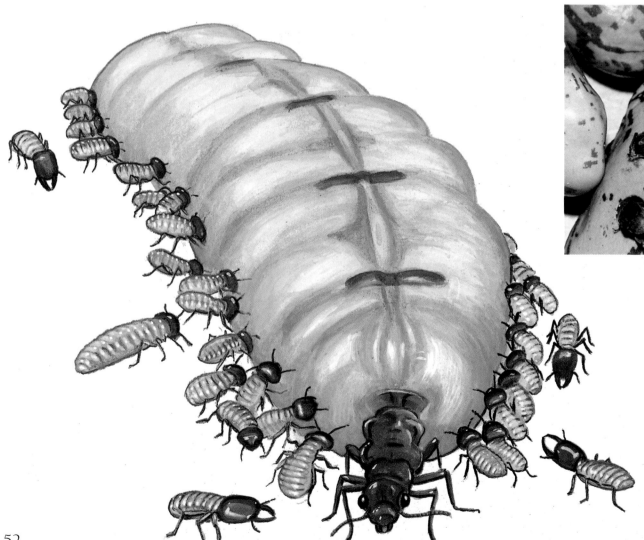

EATING FOR 40,000
Almost bursting at the seam a queen termite can lay 40,000 eggs a day. Her swollen abdomen prevents the queen from moving. Workers take over, feeding and grooming her while soldier termites patrol the nest. Organisms living in their intestines help termites digest the cellulose in wood.

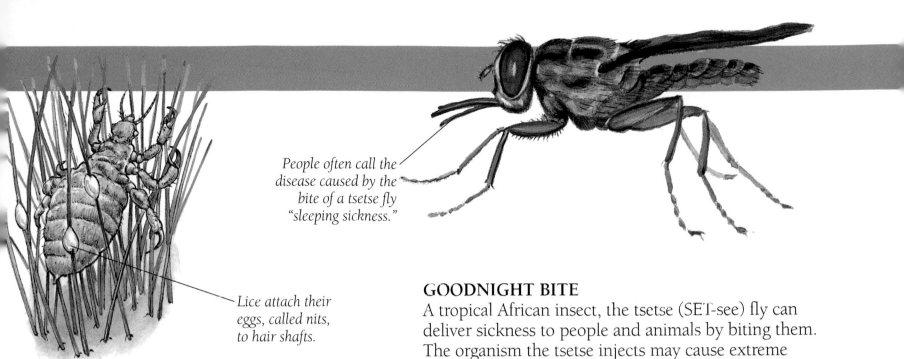

People often call the disease caused by the bite of a tsetse fly "sleeping sickness."

Lice attach their eggs, called nits, to hair shafts.

LOUSY LOUSE

The head louse is an unwelcome visitor in schools the world over. Constant head scratching announces these tiny pests that feed on human blood.

GOODNIGHT BITE

A tropical African insect, the tsetse (SET-see) fly can deliver sickness to people and animals by biting them. The organism the tsetse injects may cause extreme sleepiness in humans. That same organism makes other animals sicken and waste away.

FIRE! FIRE!

Named for their red color and painful bites, fire ants move in a mass through the water. These tiny insects inflict stings on grazing animals from the southern U.S. to South America. The ants in the swarm constantly change places so that all can breathe.

53

Insect Friends

Insects can be naughty or nice, and some are both. Cousins of the moths that munch holes in our sweaters give us silk for dresses and shirts. Bees that deliver nasty stings also give us sweet honey to enjoy. Ladybugs may "fly away home," but not before doing away with the pesky aphids that eat our roses and other plants. It's hard to imagine a world without insects.

SILKMEISTER

A silk moth perches on the cocoon it made as a caterpillar, or silkworm. Most moth caterpillars make silk, but only several species make the strands used for cloth.

Silk comes from a gland near the silkworm's mouth. The silkworm spins its silk in a continuous thread that may stretch almost 4,000 feet when unraveled. The ancient Chinese discovered silk-making and kept it a closely guarded secret for several thousand years.

Hive workers fan nectar with their wings, speeding the evaporation of moisture.

When the honey is ready, the bees cap off the cells with wax from their abdomens.

HONEY TALKS

Bees make honey from nectar they drink from flowers. They carry the nectar in their abdomens and transfer it to workers that store it in cells in the hive.

PAYING THE PRICE

Having just destroyed one tomato, a tomato hornworm caterpillar prepares to nibble another. But this garden pest is about to meet its match. A praying mantis waits for the hornworm to make one more move before it becomes a meal.

Did You Know...

1 **THAT** one kind of lantern bug tries to pass itself off as an alligator? Sticking out in front of its eyes is a miniature alligator head, complete with fake teeth. This unusual mimicry may confuse the monkeys that like to eat the insect. Another common name for this trickster is peanut bug.

2 **THAT** an ant can live after losing its head? Each segment of an ant's body contains a ganglion, a kind of brain made of nerve cells. The ganglion can keep the insect moving and doing—at least for a while—even if the head segment is missing.

3 **THAT** the nymphs of some cicadas rest for 17 years before completing the transformation to adult form? After hatching from an egg, a cicada nymph burrows into the ground. It feeds on roots and grows slowly for years until it is ready for adult life.

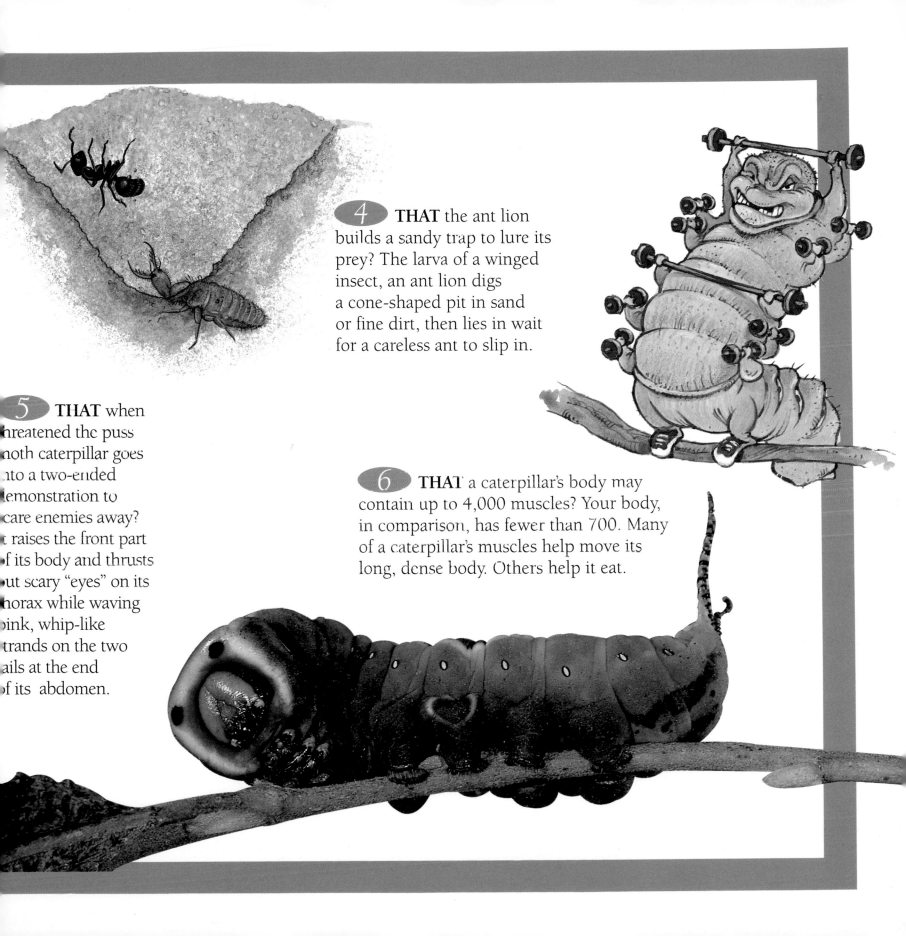

4 **THAT** the ant lion builds a sandy trap to lure its prey? The larva of a winged insect, an ant lion digs a cone-shaped pit in sand or fine dirt, then lies in wait for a careless ant to slip in.

5 **THAT** when threatened the puss moth caterpillar goes into a two-ended demonstration to scare enemies away? It raises the front part of its body and thrusts out scary "eyes" on its thorax while waving pink, whip-like strands on the two tails at the end of its abdomen.

6 **THAT** a caterpillar's body may contain up to 4,000 muscles? Your body, in comparison, has fewer than 700. Many of a caterpillar's muscles help move its long, dense body. Others help it eat.

Glossary

ABDOMEN The rear segment of an insect's body, which contains organs for digestion and reproduction.

ANTENNA One of a pair of thin, segmented organs located on the head of an insect that help it smell, feel, and taste.

CAMOUFLAGE A natural disguise, such as skin color or pattern, that helps an animal blend with its surroundings.

CHRYSALIS The resting stage of a caterpillar as it transforms into an adult butterfly.

COCOON A protective covering made by a moth caterpillar from its own silk in which it rests and transforms into an adult moth.

GRUB The thick, worm-like larva of some insects, such as beetles.

HALTERE Short, club-like structures attached to a fly's thorax that help it balance in flight. Halteres developed from a fly's rear wings.

INVERTEBRATE An animal, such as an insect, that has no backbone.

JUVENILE A young, or immature, animal.

LARVA A stage in the life of some insects after hatching from an egg. A larva looks very different from an adult.

MAGGOT The soft-bodied larva of a fly.

METAMORPHOSIS The change in structure by an animal that has more than one body form during its life.

MIMICRY Adopting the body shape and coloration of another, often more dangerous, animal to avoid predators.

Also, adopting the form and color of an object in the environment, such as a leaf or flower.

MOLTING The shedding of a too-small exoskeleton by an insect as it grows. When insects reach the adult stage, they stop growing and molting.

NYMPH A stage in the life of some insects after hatching from the egg. A nymph looks like an adult, but is smaller and lacks wings and the ability to mate.

PARASITE An organism that lives on or in another life form; a parasite gets its food from its host and often harms it

PHEROMONES Chemicals produced in the bodies of animals that send messages to members of the same species.

POLLINATION The process in which pollen is transferred from one flower to another of the same species to fertilize it—to make it produce seeds.

PREDATOR An animal that hunts and kills other animals for food.

PREY An animal that is hunted by other animals for food.

PUPA The resting stage of an insect as it transforms from larva to adult.

SPECIES A group of animals of the same kind that can produce young like themselves.

THORAX The middle segment of an insect's body, to which its legs and wings are attached.

WINGSPAN The measurement of an animal's outstretched wings from tip to tip.

ndex

ldface indicates illustrations.

nt lion **57**; trap **57**
ts **5, 7, 8, 15, 50–51, 53, 57**;
diagram of colony **48–49**; eggs
48; ganglion **56**; queens **48**
hids **7, 42, 49**
chropods **16–17**; characteristics
16
sassin bug **26–27**
as moth **4, 9**

ck swimmer **6**
an weevils **52**
ard-lichen grasshopper **22**
es **5, 7, 44–45, 46, 54, 54**
etles **5, 8, 40–43, 48**; defense
mechanisms **41, 42**; number of
species **40**
mbardier beetle **41**
aconid wasp: larvae **46**
gs **4, 26–29, 56**; characteristics
26; mimicry **56**; mouthparts **26**
lldog ant **15**; jaws **15**
tterflies **4, 7, 30–35, 60**;
camouflage **31**; chrysalis **32**;
differences from moths **30, 36**;
metamorphosis **32–33**; mouth
15; wings **30**

at fleas: jumping ability **13**
terpillars **7, 8, 32–33, 36–37,
46, 57**; eyes **12**; jaws **15**;
muscles **57**; spiracles **37**
ntipedes **16**
inese mantis **25**
inese oak silk moth **12**
nitin **10**
cadas: nymphs **56**
ear-wing butterfly **31**
ckroaches **18**; diet **18**
ickets **8, 20**; eaten by crab spider
23; jumping ability **22**;
metamorphosis **20**; nymph **20**;
singing **23**; tympanum **23**

eath's-head hawk moth **36**;

caterpillar **36–37**
Deer tick **16**
Dragonflies **6, 18**; compound eye
12; fossil **18**
Dune cricket **20**
Dung beetle **41**; nest **41**

Earwigs **4, 18**; defense
mechanisms **18**
Eighty-nine butterfly **4, 30**
Elephant hawk moth **30**
Eulophid wasps **9**

Field: cross section showing insect
life **8**
Fire ants **53**
Fireflies **42**
Fleas **13**
Flies **5, 6, 38, 39, 52, 53**; caught
by assassin bug **27**; suction pads
on feet **38**
Flower mantis **2-3, 24**
Froghoppers: nymphs **28**

Goliath beetle **40**
Grasshoppers **7, 11, 13, 22, 23**;
jumping ability **22**; singing **13,
20**; wings **11**; *see also* Katydids

Harlequin bug **26**
Head louse **52**
Hornworm caterpillar **46, 54, 55**
Houseflies **5, 38**
Hummingbird: attacked by mantis
25

Ichneumon wasp **46**
Insects: antennae **11**; beneficial role
54; body segments **10, 11**;
camouflage **20, 22**;
characteristics **6**; exoskeleton **10,
20**; feeding methods **14**; habitats
8; meat-eating **24**; mimicry **20,
38, 56**; mouthparts **14**; nymphs
28; pollination **44**; warning
colors **23**; wings **11, 18**

Katydids **4, 20-21, 22**; camouflage

20, 21; jumping ability **22**

Lacewings, green **1**
Ladybird beetles **6, 42, 43**; aphid
predation **42, 54**; emerging from
pupa **42**
Ladybird mimic beetles **5, 43**
Ladybugs *see* Ladybird beetles
Lantern bug **56**
Leaf butterfly **31**
Leaf katydid **4, 20–21**
Leaf mantis **25**
Leafcutter ants **5, 50–51**;
destruction of rain forest trees
51; underground nests **51**
Lice **52**
Lichen walkingstick **24**
Lyme disease **16**

Maggot **38**
Mantises **2–3, 12, 24, 24–25, 54,
55**; with prey **25**
Midge: trapped in amber **18, 19**
Millipede **16**
Mite: trapped in amber **18, 19**
Monarch butterflies **34–35**;
caterpillar **32–33**; diet **33**;
metamorphosis **32–33**;
migration **34, 35**, map **35**;
tagging **34**
Mosquitoes **6, 14, 52**; female
sucking human blood **14**;
mouthparts **14**
Moths **4, 9, 30, 36, 37, 54**;
antennae **12, 36**; caterpillar
36–37; defense mechanisms **9**;
differences from butterflies **30,
36**; mating **36**; metamorphosis
32, 33; pheromones **36**; pupa
32; wings **8, 30**
Mud daubers (wasps) **5, 46, 47**;
nests **46**

Parasol ants *see* Leafcutter ants
Peanut bug **56**
Potter wasp **46**; nest **46**
Praying mantises **7, 12, 24, 25, 55**;
vision **12**

Puss moth caterpillar **57**; defense
mechanism **57**

Rat-tailed maggot **38**

Scorpion **17**
Shield bugs **28**; eggs **28**; nymphs
28–29
Silk moths **12, 54**
Silkworms **54**
Sleeping sickness **53**
Spiders **16, 23**; body segments **16**
Spiny katydid **23**
Spittlebugs **28**
Springtails **8**
Stag beetle **7, 41**
Stinkbugs **26, 28**; eggs **29**
Syrphid fly **39**; immature **38**;
mimicry **39**

Termites: digestion process **52**;
queen swollen with eggs **52**
Ticks **16**
Tsetse fly **53**
Two-striped grasshopper **13**

Walkingstick **24**
Wasps **5, 9, 46–47**; characteristics
46; larvae **46**
Water boatman **13**
Water bug **4**; carrying eggs on back
28
Water strider **26**
Weevils **40, 52**
Wolf spider **16**; pedipalps **16**

Yellow dung fly **38**

Credits

ruby lacewing butterfly

Published by
The National Geographic Society
Reg Murphy, *President
   and Chief Executive Officer*
Gilbert M. Grosvenor,
   Chairman of the Board
Nina D. Hoffman,
   Senior Vice President
William R. Gray, *Vice President and Director, Book Division*

Staff for this Book
Barbara Lalicki, *Director of Children's Publishing*
Barbara Brownell, *Senior Editor and Project Manager*
Marianne R. Koszorus, *Senior Art Director and Project Manager*
Toni Eugene, *Editor*
Alexandra Littlehales, *Art Director*
Sally Collins, *Illustrations Editor*
Catherine Herbert Howell, *Researcher*
Meredith Wilcox, *Illustrations Assistant*
Dale-Marie Herring, *Editorial Assistant*
Elisabeth MacRae-Bobynskyj, *Indexer*
Mark A. Caraluzzi, *Marketing Manager*
Vincent P. Ryan, *Manufacturing Manager*

Acknowledgments

We are grateful for the assistance of Dr. David W. Inouye, Department of Zoology, University of Maryland; Dr. David D. Yager, Department of Psychology, University of Maryland, and Dr. Lincoln P. Brower, University of Florida, *Scientific Consultants*. We also thank John Agnone and Rebecca Lescaze, National Geographic Book Division, for their guidance and suggestions.

Illustrations Credits

Cover: Robert and Linda Mitchell.
Interior photos from Animals Animals/Earth Scenes:
Front Matter: 1 Stephen Dalton/OSF. 2-3 Michael Fogden. 4 (top to bottom), Jack J. De Coningh; J. Robinson; Michael Fogden; John Lemker; OSF. 5 (top to bottom), Avril Ramage/OSF; G.I. Bernard/OSF; Stephen Dalton/OSF; G.I. Bernard; M.A. Chappell. 6-7 (art), Warren Cutler. 8 (art), Robert Cremins 9 Jack J. De Coningh. 10 (art), Warren Cutler. 11 Stephen Dalton. 12 (art), Warren Cutler. 12 (upper), Alastair Shay/OSF. 12 (left), Michael P. Gadomski. 12 (right), E.R. Degginger. 13 (art), Warren Cutler. 13 (upper), Stephen Dalton. 13 (lower), Donald Specker. 14 (art), Warren Cutler. 14 OSF. 15 (art), Warren Cutler. 15 (both), Kathie Atkinson/ OSF. 16 (art), Robert Cremins. 16 Zig Leszczynski. 17 (art), Robert Cremins. 17 (upper), E.R. Degginger. 17 (lower) Raymond A. Mendez.
Ancient Insects: 18 (art), Robert Cremins. 18 (upper), E.R. Degginger. 18 (center), J.H. Robinson. 18 (lower), Michael Dick. 19 Raymond A. Mendez.
Crickets and Grasshoppers: 20 (art), Warren Cutler. 20 Anthony Bannister. 20-21 Michael Fogden. 22 (art), Robert Cremins. 22 (upper) Richard K. La Val. 22 (lower), Doug Wechsler. 23 (left), Kjell Sandved/OSF. 23 (right), Richard Kolar.
Mantises: 24 (left), Michael Fogden. 24 (right), Paul Freed. 25 (left), Jack Wilburn. 25 (art), Warren Cutler. 25 (upper), P.&W. Ward/OSF. 25 (lower), Bill Beatty.
Bugs: 26 (art), Warren Cutler. 26 Kathie Atkinson/OSF. 26-27 J.H. Robinson. 28 (art), Robert Cremins. 28 (upper), John Lemker. 28 (center), Raymond A. Mendez. 28-29 K.G. Preston-Mafham. 29 Maria Zorn.
Butterflies and Moths: 30 (art), Robert Cremins. 30 (left), G.I. Bernard. 30 (right), OSF. 30-31 Stephen Dalton. 31 (left), E.R. Degginger. 31 (right), Patti Murray. 32 (upper), J.A.L. Cooke/OSF. 32 (lower), 32-33, 34 Patti Murray. 33 (art), Robert Cremins. 35 (art), Robert Cremins. 35 M.A. Chappell. 36 (upper), B.G. Murray, Jr. 36 (lower), OSF. 36-37 Alastair Shay/OSF. 37 (art), Robert Cremins.
Flies: 38 (art), Robert Cremins. 38 (center), Stephen Dalton/OSF. 38 (left), Avril Ramage/OSF. 38 (right), G.I. Bernard/OSF. 39 D.R. Specker.
Beetles: 40 (art), Warren Cutler. 40 K.G. Preston-Mafham. 41 (art), Warren Cutler. 41 E.R. Degginger. 42 (art), Robert Cremins. 42 (center), J.H. Robinson. 42 (lower), Robert Maier. 43 (left), Bates Littlehales. 43 (right), G.I. Bernard/OSF.
Bees and Wasps: 44 (upper), Fritz Prenzel. 44 (lower), D.R. Specker. 45 (art), Robert Cremins. 45, (upper), OSF. 46 (art, upper), Warren Cutler. 46 (art, lower), Warren Cutler. 46 (lower), Patti Murray. 47 Stephen Dalton/OSF.
Ants: 48-49 (art), Warren Cutler. 50 J.A.L. Cooke/OSF. 51 (lower), Michael Dick. 51 (upper), G.I. Bernard.
Good and Bad Insects: (art, left), Warren Cutler. 52 (art, right), Robert Cremins. 52 Michael Gadomski. 53 (art), Warren Cutler. 53 C. C. Lockwood. 54 (art), Warren Cutler. 54 (upper), G. I. Bernard/OSF. 54 (lower), M.A. Chappell. 54-55 Zig Leszczynski.
Back Matter: 56 (art), Robert Cremins. 56 Michael Fogden. 57 (art), Robert Cremins. 57 OSF. 60 K.G. Cole.

COVER: A praying mantis rises on its rear legs, raises its front legs, and extends its wings to scare off enemies. Mantises perform such displays when threatened.

Composition for this book by the National Geographic Society Book Division. Printed and bound by R.R. Donnelley & Sons Company, Willard, Ohio. Color separations by Quad Graphics, Martinsburg, West Virginia. Case cover printed by Inland Press, Menomonee Falls, Wisconsin.

Library of Congress CIP Data
Howell, Catherine Herbert.
   Insects / by Catherine Herbert Howell.
      p.   cm   —   (National Geographic nature library)
   Includes index.
   Summary: Discusses the physical characteristics of insects and examines different kinds, including crickets, butterflies, and wasps.
      ISBN 0-7922-7044-4
      1. Insects—Juvenile literature.   [1. Insects.]   I. Title.
   II. Series.
   QL467.2H7   1997
   595.7.6—dc21
                                                    97-14561
                                                    CIP
                                                    AC